UIESH

SOMEWHERE

Also by Joséphine Bacon

A Tea in the Tundra / Nipishapui nete mushuat
(translated by Donald Winkler)

Message Sticks / Tshissinuatshitakana
(translated by Phyllis Aronoff)

UIESH
SOMEWHERE

POEMS

Joséphine Bacon

Dual-language edition in Innu-aimun and English

TRANSLATED FROM THE FRENCH
BY JESSICA MOORE

TALONBOOKS

Talonbooks
9259 Shaughnessy Street, Vancouver, British Columbia, Canada v6p 6r4
talonbooks.com

Talonbooks is located on xʷməθkʷəy̓əm, Sḵwx̱wú7mesh, and səlilwətaɬ Lands.

First printing: 2024

Typeset in Minion
Printed and bound in Canada on 100% post-consumer recycled paper

Talonbooks acknowledges the financial support of the Canada Council for the Arts, the Government of Canada through the Canada Book Fund, and the Province of British Columbia through the British Columbia Arts Council and the Book Publishing Tax Credit.

This work was originally published bilingually in Innu-aimun and French as *Uiesh / Quelque part* by Mémoire d'encrier, Montréal, Québec, in 2018. We acknowledge the financial support of the Government of Canada through the National Translation Program for Book Publishing, an initiative of the *Roadmap for Canada's Official Languages 2013–2018: Education, Immigration, Communities*, for our translation activities.

Library and Archives Canada Cataloguing in Publication

Title: Uiesh = Somewhere : poems / Joséphine Bacon ; dual-language edition in the original Innu-aimun and English ; translated from the French by Jessica Moore.
Other titles: Somewhere
Names: Bacon, Joséphine, 1947- author | Moore, Jessica, 1978- translator | Container of (work): Bacon, Joséphine, 1947- Uiesh. | Container of (expression): Bacon, Joséphine, 1947- Uiesh. English.
Description: Poetry originally written in Innu-aimun. Previously published in a bilingual Innu-aimun/French edition. This edition is bilingual Innu-aimun/English. English text translated from the French.
Identifiers: Canadiana 20240431766 | ISBN 9781772015140 (softcover)
Subjects: LCGFT: Poetry.
Classification: LCC PS8603.A3343 U5413 2024 | DDC C897/.32—dc23

Prologue

Today, I am somewhere in my life.

I belong to the race of Elders. I want to be a
poet in the Oral Tradition, to speak like the
Ancient Innu, the true nomads. I have not
walked Nutshimit, the Land.

They have told it to me. I have listened to the
story of my origins. They baptized me in water
from a pure lake.

One by one, the Elders are leaving us. With
them go the words of the tundra, the currents
of the rivers, the calm of the lakes.

I feel I inherit their words, their stories, their
nomadic way of life. Like them, I have walked
the tundra, I have honoured the caribou.

Somewhere, a stone on a larger stone marks
my presence.

—JOSÉPHINE BACON

Uiesh

Apu tapue utshimashkueupaniuian pemuteiani
Anikashkau nishpishkun miam tshiashishkueu
Nuatshikaten
Miam ishkueu ka pakatat
Miam ishkueu ka peshuat auassa pemuteti

Somewhere

I don't sashay like a cat
my back is the bent back
of the Ancestors
my legs the bowed legs
of women who portaged
women who gave birth
while walking

Nuapateti eshpitenitakuak nutin
Nuapaten eshpish minuashit
Nitakussinik^u nutin

Nikamuitik
Nipa minuenitamuan tutamuk unikamun

I live wide as the wind
feel its beauty

Wind takes me in its arms

whistles a melody
I want to write

Tshitshisseniten nishimish
Apu auen tshimutit ka ishi-takuak
Tshishik^u
Ishkuteu
Nipi

Apu auen tshi tshimutit assinu
Anite ka inniuin

Apu auen tshi tshimutit
Ueshinamini

You know, little brother
no one steals

The elements are human
air person
fire person
water person

No one can steal
the Land
that saw your birth

No one can steal
your smile

Mishau aimun ua minitan
Nitshishenniun
Nushitshikueuna

Anutshish apu tshishkapataian
Ninute-nenen
Nishaputueten nipuamunit

Nipeten nipisha
Nitshishkutamatishun inniun
Nitshisheishkueun nuitsheukun

Apu 100 itaki aimuna manitan
Apu 100 itati-pipuneshian

I have a hundred words to tell you
the story of my old age
my wrinkles

Gone, my lightness of foot

Short of breath now
but in my dreaming I walk on
tireless

I know how to hear the leaves
I learn the world
my age grows old with me

I haven't got a hundred words
I haven't lived a hundred years

Ka tshinuapekak tetapuakan nitapin unuitamit
Uasheshkupanu
Mitshinanushu nimashinaikan
Uapinushiu nimashinaikanashk^u

Niminuenimun
Kashikat nitshisheishkueun
Aimuna nipatshitinen
Tshishennuat ka miniht

Nin kuessipan

Public bench
reluctant sun
pink notebook
grey pen and
my dog watching me

A small happiness creeps up
My old age settles in
I have words to pass on
stories from the Elders

Everything turns
it's my turn now

Niminuten shatshitun-aimuna
Apu pishkapamin
Tshitshisseniten eka uiapamin
Anite iaitapin

Nitatshakush apu nukushit
Tshinanatuapamau uiesh
Tshinanatuapaten nitei
Tshinikamun

Tshinikumin
Tshinikumin

My head spins with tender words
You don't notice me
you see my absence
in the image you've created

Behind my invisible spirit
you seek the place
you seek the heart
you take up the song

you take up the song
you take up the song

Nui shikuanitan
Kun apu ui apashit
Mashk^u, nimushum apishikushu
Pipun mitshimishkam^u

I live in a winter springtime
snow holds back its season

The bear, my grandfather
wakes

Winter presses on

Parc Molson nititan
Matueshtin
Katakushish petakushuat kaiashtueitsheshiht
Akushiutapan petakuan

Apu tshi nishataman tshetshi kau
tshissitutaman
Ka minuataman ka ishi-petaman
Tshishennuat tepatshimutaui
Assi e nenemakak

Parc Molson
a light breeze rustles the trees
Far off, fire engines
an ambulance

I can't help returning
to the sounds I love
voices of Elders
vibrations of the earth

Nitshishkuepanitishun
Anite tipatshimunissit
Apu tshekuan petakuak
Uanasse tshimashinaimatin

Tshuapamitin innitsheuanit

I get drunk on
sentences
silences
to write you

my vision is image

Petapan
Kakuenimeu
Akaushinua ka tshikuanishkashk^u

Nimamituneniten
Tatuetakanu anite etaian
Tshitaikanitak nikamun
Utat nakana ninatuapamakun

Nunitshissituten eshi-puamunan
Kashikat nitei uni-tshissitutam^u ka
tshikashamet
Nitapueten tshetshi utinikuian
Shash nitishpan

Tshipetatin tshiman
Tanite tshetshi uitshitan
Nipa minueniten nikamututaman
Tshikassenitamun
Minitan utshekatak^u tshetshi kau ushinamin

Every red dawn is jealous
of the eclipse that's been
all over you

A thought swallows me
clamour of a night at the bar
a melody sings my memory
the past catches up

I've forgotten how to dream
my heart has lost the rhythm of snowshoes
I've let myself be tamed
I'm at the end of me

I listen to your tears
(how can I console you)
I want to chase away your pain
give you the smile of a star

Amassepanu shikuan mak pipun
Apateu
Pipun ui tau

Tshishennu nashpitutueu nutina
Uteshkan-pineua apatshieu
Nasht nitshishkuaik
Ekue eka nukushit nakana

Tshititutein pakatakan-meshkanat
Tshunashinatauau nutin
Tshinashatin
Nitshitapaten mashinaikanashk^u

Unashinataim^u
Tshitipenitamunnu

Today spring has mixed with winter
everything melts
winter hasn't had its last word

An Elder mimics the wind
He bewitches me
with partridge wings
then disappears

You lead me down a path
you write in the wind
I follow behind
I watch the pencil draw light lines
of your freedom

Nuapateti ussi-pipun
Tshiam mishpunipan
Kunissat utshekatakuipanat
Ute umenu assinu ka piuenitakannit
Peikuan minakupan
Tshiashinnua

I saw the birth of winter

in a tortured world
snow abandons its fragile flakes

Their fineness dazzles
the Land of nomads

Nitshipauitishun utenat
Apu uapataman tshishik^u
Nitituten anite tshissishikua
Eshi-atishauiateti
Nitatshakush uashtepanu

I lock myself up in a city
deprived of a horizon
I move towards your eyes
their colour
lays bare
my spirit

Ninanatuapaten aimuniss
Anite kashekau-aimunit

Nitshitapaten e itashtain

Nitepuen
Tshetshi tain

I'm looking for the word in the poem

I read you

I invoke
your presence

Tshuapamititi ka inniuin
Namaieu tshin tshetshishepaushu
Tshin an puamun
Tshimin
Tshiaminniun

I saw your birth
you are not the morning
you are the dream
You give me the illusion
of peace

Mishta-utshekataku uashku
Tshitipatshimushtakunu
Mishta-utshekatakua
Uashtuashkun nimu assit

Ume tipishkau
Eukuan ka tshitshenanut
Tshikashinamakunan

A night of stars invites us in
tells us the story
of the Great Bear

The Northern Lights
dance the movements of the Land

Tonight is the night of the scars
that forgive

Nitapashtan tipishkau tshetshi kassenitaman
Nitapashtan tipishkau tshetshi mashinaimatan
Nitapashtan tipishkau tshetshi inniuian
Nitapashtan kashikau tshetshi inniuian
Nitapashtan nakana utat tshetshi eka
unitshissian
Uapaki apu tshissenitaman

I need the night for sadness
I need the night to write you
I need life to live
I need the present to be
I need the past to go on
Tomorrow has no notion of me

Namaieu nin uapan
Nin aum kashikau
Nitei kau tshiuepanu
Tepatshimushtuini nitipatshimun

Nin aum tshukum pishim^{u}
Ka pimipanit
Memenishpun
Tshitshishkuein
Kau natetau tshiashi-inniun

I am not tomorrow
I am today
My heart turns over
in space
when you tell my story

I am the big moon
moving through time
Swirl of snow
I lose my head
May tradition live on

Nipapun nipimakan
Apu tshekuan petakuak
Akuitishun shashtiku
Kau takuan mitunenitshikan
Eshpitishian nikushpaneniten kashinamatun

My laughter dies
splinters of silence
pain spits
consciousness returns

My age frets
over forgiveness

Nititan anite aimuna ka tutaman
Nitshishpeuaushun apu petak
nitshishuapunnu
Apu tshi tipatshimunanut ninekatenitamun
Apu shakutaian

Anite ka akua-tipishkat nitituten
Tshetshi tshissenitaman tanite uetuteian

Tshetshi mishkatishuian
Anite ka tipatshimitishuian

Apu tshissenimin etaian

Aimunit ninipin

I exist in the words I write
fighting in a quiet rage
My pain cannot be told
My battle gives up the ghost

I go to the ends of the night
to find the best version of myself

to reach myself
there, where I tell the story of myself

You don't even know I exist

I die in a single word

Namaieu nin nanimissuat
Nin aum assi ka matshit

Teueikan nitituteik
Nuash nete
Mishta-pakatakan

I am not thunder
I am movement of the earth

The drum guides me
to the path
of the Great Portage

Shakassineu tipishkau-pishim^u
Utshekatakuat nukushuat
Ishpimit nitaitapin
Miam nin uashtenamutau
Nitatshakush pimishipaniu
Kun uashtenam^u

The whole moon
the stars are here
Eyes on the sky
I like to think they shine for me

My shadow stretches long
Snow is radiant light

Nitshissitutuau Shuaushemiss
Nimushum kanataut
Eshk^u kashikanit nuapamau ashit uteueikana
Ishkueua katsheshkaimueu
Kukuminasha
Shuaushemiss minuaneu uteueikana
Nitshitapamik^u ekue mishta-ushinak
Kukuminasha ka katsheshkaimuat
Unatau-assi katsheshkaimushapan
E kununiti
E nutiki
Memenishpun

I remember Shuaushemiss
Grandfather Hunter
I see him again with his drum
He sings a woman with white hair
His song spurs on the dance
Shuaushemiss sets the drum down tenderly
looks at me and bursts out laughing
The woman with white hair
is his hunting grounds
covered in snow
Wind picks up and
she whirls

Nuapamati ishkuessiss anite mishtikut,
baobab ka inan
Uashteshiu
Akushumu pishim^u e uapamati
Takunam^u ushashkuteun
Uauitam^u matau-aimuna

I've seen the daughter of the baobab
she is light
The sun slips away
Her talking stick
shares words of mystery

Tshishkueienitakuan
Piputeshtin tshishkuepanitau assinu
Apu nukushit pishim^u
Nutineteu kau natuapatam^u shakaikana
Nipimutaik^u pipun
Nitshikutina pashpapuakana
Apu tshikanaman eshpish uapishit kun
Apu uapataman anite ka takusseian
Nutin nana uepashtatau
Kashkuannu
Nitapishkatshen mitshet ka ishi-atishauianit
Nitapishkakan
Minu-tshishikau niteit
Ueuepashuat kunissat

Weather grows unhinged
Blowing snow, you stun the earth
The sun gives way
Nutineteu* has seized the river
with his mist
I walk the winter
Frost sets in on windows
Blinding whiteness
I can't find my tracks
Wind has carried them off
in a single cloud
My scarf of many colours
brightens the weather
makes the flakes pirouette

---

* In Innu-aimun, the mist on the snow in very cold
temperatures; a personification of extreme cold.

Apu ut tipatshimatau nitshinnuat
Apu ut uauitamin nitinniunan
Apu ut natutamin ka itueiat
Ninikamunan
Anite teueikanit
Tshetshi shaputue puamuiat

You haven't told the story of my people
You haven't spoken of our existence
You haven't heard our voice

Voice singing an incantation
in the skin of the drum
so the dream will go on

Mishau aimun e nenekatenitakaniti
Shutshishimakana
Animan inniun
E kassenitakaniti

Unashkut
Apu nukuak e uasheiashtet

Sometimes pain is a muse
dictates words
full of power

Life struggles to live
strung up in suffering

In the end
the light won't light anymore

Tshitshinikuanishkun
Tshin ka tipatshimin
Tshituten tshetshi ui taian

Eka anueta

Nimashinatein
Ute e taian

You orbit around me
you who tell the story of my life

Here in the spinning, I strive to exist

Don't keep denying

I am writing
my presence

Uiesh
Ute utenat
Anutshish
Nin aum innu

Ninanatuapaten anite ka mitameian

Somewhere
in this city
I am the human
of the moment

looking for my tracks

Nimushumat pimutatamupanat nutshimit
Nukumat uapamaushuipanat nikauinana
Ekuta uetshian
Manenitakanu nitassi
Atshinepik^{u} umatshi-natukunim patshitinam^{u}
Anite ka pimukut tshitipatshimunnu

My grandfathers travelled the Land
My grandmothers gave birth to our mothers
I come from the tradition of spoken words

My Land is being violated
by a poisonous snake

there, where my history flows

Ninanipaun Bélanger meshkanat
Nitashuapaten netupiss
Nitshitapaten tanite nuash e itamut
meshkanau
Apu uapataman tshishik^u

Nipashikuapan
Nuapamauat unaman-shipiu-tshishennuat
Ushtishkupishtamuat uinipekunu
Uinuau muk^u uapatamuat
Ka tshipatahk

Rue Bélanger
waiting for the bus
looking down the road
with no horizon

I close my eyes and find
the Elders from Unamen-shipu
sitting facing the ocean

Only they see
what they see

Aieshkushiuimakan inniun
Pakushenitamun ashuapu
Nitatinen nitshishenakushiuna
Peiku-pipuna eshk^u nui inniun
Ekuta ute e nakauian
Nitishpiteniten nitei

A tired life
hope suspended

My finger traces another wrinkle
for another year

I stop my rush
and honour a slow heart

Tshimitshimiuan utakupit
Tshimatishueniten inniun
Kashekau-aimuna tipatshimuat
E nutepanin shatshitun

Tshin an nutshimiu-auass
Ka uepinakanit

Tshui nishtuapamakuan
Tshushimun
Shipu tshitashuapamik^{u}

You cling to an invisible skirt
unsure about existence
Words tell of your lack
of love

Son of a Land that abandons you

To know yourself
you run away

A river awaits your return

Kau tipishkau
Nitashuapaten tshetshi nutekushian
Tshika takushin a nipuamunit
Tshetshi petuk tshiteueikan
Nimiani nitinniunit

Another night
I lie waiting for sleep

Will you come in my dream
Will you play the drum
make my life get up and dance

Utshekatakuat tshuauinauat
Shipua tshuauitamatin
Ka ishi-takuak tshishikut tshuauiten
Shakaikana tshuauitamatin
Eshpitashkamikat tshuauiten
Mushuau-assi tshuauitamatin
Anisheniuat tshuauinauat
Uashtuashkuan tshuauitamatin
Uashku tshuauiten
Nutshimiu tshuauitamatin

You speak of stars
I tell you about rivers
You speak of planets
I tell you about lakes
You speak of the infinite
I tell you about the tundra
You speak of angels
I tell you about the Northern Lights
You speak of the heavens
I tell you about the Land

Mishta-tshitutenanu
Apu uishamikauian

Natinen nitashtamik^u apu matenitaman
Nitashuapaten tshetshi tshishenniuian

Nakana anite ka tipatshimikuin

Departures
I'm not invited

I wait for the lines on my face
caress in empty space

a story of you

Tshimin tipaikan
Tshinatuenitamatin tshishik^u
Nutinen nishashkauteun
Tshinashatin
Apu tshi tsheshtipititan
Usham ninikatishin

You give me a second
I ask for a moment
Your steps are in a rush
I'm looking for my cane
to follow

My slowness separates me
from you

Namaieu tshin eka ka petakuak
Tshin an ka peikutat aimunnu
Tshin eka kueshte ka aimit
Tshitshisseniten kassinu tshekuan
essishuemakak
Apu tshitapatamin tipaipishimuan
E tshikashteti unitau ka tshishipanishiniti
Tshinanipaun
Tshiashinnuat tshuapamikuat
Namaieu tshin atshakush

You are no longer silence
you are synonym
antonym
You know their definition
You don't watch the clock

Hours pass
minutes lose their seconds

Standing upright
the Elders see you
you are not a mirage

Insistence on
the present →
while reaching
in to the past +
future.

Nimaunapuia
Apu ashte-utshikuniti
Anite tshe tshimuak

The tears of my life
take anchor in
this forecast rain

Nushitshikuen anumat
Nukuan nitinniun nitashtamikut
Nukuan ka ishinniuian
Kashikat nikukuminashiun
Nitipatshimun

I have so many lines on my face
Each one
has lived my life

Today I am the noble woman
who tells the story

Nunishen nitshissitutamuna
Nitakussutan niat

Minupeiashu shakaikan
Nuapamitishun
Nin aum innushkueu nuash nimukuiapit
Nin aum innushkueu anite niteit

Nitatshakush unipanu nanikutini
Nitinniun tshishenniumakan e petuki
teueikan
Anite nipuamunit

I have cut out my memories
glued them to my body.

A calm lake
reflects the image of me
Innu in my veins
Innu in my red heart

My shadow merges with my spirit
My life grows old to the sound
of the drum in my dreams

Kassinu tshekuan e inniuimakak tshimin
Tipishkau-pishim^u e uauieshit

Nuishamikaun anite e tauapekaitshenanut
Shash nitshi petenashapan
Nititinamakaun kashutshishimakak
Nitashuapaten kashekau-aimun

Universe, you offer up
a full round moon

I'm greeted with a tune
I've heard before
A hand holds out a Scotch
I wait for them to listen to the poem

Eka ui nipai usham nitinniun
Eka ui nipai usham nushinen
Eka ui nipai usham ut shatshitun
Eka ui nipai usham innu aum nin

Nipaii
Uni-tshissitutamani

Don't kill me for being alive
Don't kill me for smiling
Don't kill me for loving
Don't kill me for being human

Kill me
if I forget

Apu tshishuapian usham e tshishenniuian
Apu tshishuapishtaman inniun
Apu tshissenitaman tshe ishpish nakataman
assi
Takuan nanikutini
Nuimueshtateniten nana
Nipa ishi-puamuti

I don't blame life
for growing old
I don't know the hour
of my departure
Some mornings
I long for dreams
I haven't dreamed

Nupinen nititshi
Nin natupanu ka kashimut
Apu petakuaki nimaunapuia
Nin aum natau-assi
Tshitututi
Nin aum tshissitutamun

Fist in the air
warrior in soundless tears
I am territory
you have built me
I am remembrance
you continue my education

Tanite nakanat pipun-pishimuat
Ka auassiuian

Uetakussit nipeikussin

Apu mashinaitsheian uapaki
Kashikat nimashinaitshen

Tshimuan unuitimit
Ute tshititan

Where have they gone, the nine months of
winter
from my childhood

Tonight I am alone

I don't write tomorrow
I write today

You're here
with the rain

Nuitsheuakan nipu
Nikasseniten
Nitshishuapin
Ishinakuan tshetshi shutshiteieian
Tshetshi eka akuikuian
Ishinakuan tshetshi shaputue inniuian
Eka tati
Unuitshikuna nissishikua
Auat tshemuaki
Apu ishpishipeiat

I'm sad
my friend is leaving me
Hate comes easily with departures
need courage in my pain
I have to bear your absence

My eyes release their tears
even the rain has never cried so much

Kun tshuaushinak^u
Kun nuaushinak^u
Lac Simon
Nimateniten niat
Nuapaten nikan
Nitshishuapun apu petakuak

The snow mocks you
The snow mocks me
Lac Simon trembles my life
Visions trouble the future
My anger becomes silence

Mishue nimitametan
Shipit nutshinan
Atshinepik^u ka itenitakuak
Tshitshitapekamutan

Ishkuteu neshtaputau e mamatueiat

Our steps have left their trace
We belong to a river

Inside us
you bury
an iron snake

A fire drowns out our wailing

Nipeikupatashinan mishta-meshkanat 138
Mikuashtueu tipishkau-pishim^u
Uin nuashtenamakunan

We are alone on Route 138
a red sun night
our only light

Nin nitishkueun
Nin nukaumaun
Nin nushimimaun
Nin numishimaun
Nin nuitsheuakanimaun
Nin nuitimushikaun

Apu anu natuenitaman

I am woman
mother
sister
friend
lover

It is enough

Ishkuaiet pishimuss
Unuitimit nititan
Tshek nipeten mush ka petaman
Auenitshenat anat, nishkat piminauat
Niminueniten tapue uiapamakau
Miam atamishkakauian

Min kutakat nuapamauat pemipaniht
Nikasseniten
Minekash kashti-tipishkau
Uitakanu tshe tshishkueienitakuak
Mishau nikushpanenitamun

Nitau uieshitshemakan eshi-tshishikat

End of December, outside
a sound I recognize
My eyes seek out the sky

A flight of geese
I am spoiled, happy
Another flight of geese
and I flood with sadness
The nights are long
a storm is coming
my disquiet

The climate cheats the weather

Nishk tshin nukum
Tshitshitapamin
Tshitshitapamatin
Tshunishin
Miam nin
Utenat e taiani
Apu petaman shipu e pimikut

Grandmother goose
you look at me
I look at you
You are lost
just like me
when I'm in the city
I can't hear the river anymore

Nikanueniten aimunissa
Tshui minitin
Tshe tipatshimuin
Anite kashekau-aimunit

I have simple words
to offer
in the poem
you're telling

Ninipepin
Metikat aimitak
Mitshiminam^u e tipishkanit
Nipa minuenitenashapan minuenimuian
Nimateniten e inniuian
Muk^u anite anu ianimak
Ekuta shuk shuk
Anite inniunit

Insomnia
murmurs
to hold back
the night
I imagine myself
alive
The hardest moment
is often
life

Nipa minueniten
Kau uapataman uashtessiu

Apu tshekuan kataian
Anutshish e tshisheishkueuian

Kau mini
Kutak pipun

To see again the light
of autumn

I have no secrets to keep
in the twilight of my life

O grant me
another season

Tshutinen aimunissa
Anite e shaputuepanit aimun
Tshikanueniten e uinikauin
Tshetshi minu-tshishtapaniti

Tshima tshitaimun
Kashekau-aimit

You accept words
beyond the sentences
You take your subject
for an object

May your word be
your poem

Uiesh

Nutshimit

Nitshinat nititan

Apu atshitashunashtet

Anite epian

Nimeshkanam Pakatakan ishinikateu

Uapaki nika akutueshtinuain

Nika natain nitshissinuatshitakana

Uiesh

Nutshimit

Uiesh

Eshpitashkamikat

Assi

Somewhere
in Nutshimit
I am home
with no real address
My street is called portage route
Tomorrow I'll head back upriver
to find my message sticks
somewhere
in Nutshimit
somewhere
the grandeur
of the Land

Translator's Afterword

Joséphine Bacon's poetry calls us to a pause, an inward turning. Her plainspoken lines are as spacious as the Land she invokes – open, snowy, still. To live inside her words for a time (the shadowed, mysterious time of translation) is to go in with "a slow heart." To name the winter. To name the pain and the presence of life. It is a true honour to translate this poet, carrier of the stories of Innu Elders, and Elder herself.

I am grateful to live and work on Treaty 13 Territory. As a descendant of immigrants from Ireland and England, I grew up bounded by the concrete of Tkaronto/Toronto and spent many years in Tio:tia'ke/Montréal. I have not walked the tundra. But Bacon's words evoke in me a felt sense of the longing that flows through these poems for the peace of rivers and wide-open spaces.

With "simple words" (not always easier in translation) Joséphine Bacon carries us through and beyond the horizonless city. She offers up her way of seeing, "learn[ing] the world" and leaning in to "hear the leaves." I have leaned in to the poems and thought about how impossible it is to translate poetry at all. Poetry is made of image, sound and rhythm, and something out of reach, something that reaches inside us. Image can be offered safe passage from one language to the next. But sound and rhythm will almost always be entirely new. We see this with the poems in Innu-aimun – even if they don't know the meaning of the words, readers can grasp that their shape and sound are wholly different than in English or French. So here are some new faces of the poems. I'm grateful for the intimate space of translation, the chance to see and sense through the words and inner world of another. It is my hope that the mysterious fourth element, that *something out of reach*, is present in these versions as well.

I am thankful to my own elders, in life and in the world of literary translation, for all they have shared with me.

—JESSICA MOORE

JESSICA MOORE is an author and literary translator. Her first book, *Everything, now* (Brick Books, 2012) is a love letter to the dead and a conversation with her translation of the poetic novel *Turkana Boy* (Talonbooks, 2012) by Jean-François Beauchemin, for which she won a PEN America Translation Award. *The Whole Singing Ocean* (Nightwood, 2020) is a true story blending long poem, investigation, sailor slang, and ecological grief and was longlisted for the League of Canadian Poets' Raymond Souster Award. Her translations have been nominated for the International Booker Prize and the French-American Translation Prize, won the Wellcome Book Prize, and been featured on *Vanity Fair*'s Top Twenty and the *New York Times*'s Top Ten lists. Jessica is also a mother, a gardener, and a songwriter. She lives on Treaty 13 Territory, near the shores of Lake Ontario, that inland sea.

Renowned Innu poet, storyteller, and filmmaker JOSÉPHINE BACON was born in 1947 in Pessamit, Nitassinan. An icon of Québec literature, she writes in Innu-aimun and French and has spent her life as an ambassador for Innu language, culture, Oral Traditions, and history, sharing the wisdom and knowledge of her language and her Elders.

Bacon spent her early years on the Land with her family, living a nomadic life and listening to the Traditional Stories passed down from her Ancestors. At the age of four, she was sent to residential school in Mani-utenam (Maliotenam), where she remained until she was nineteen. By collaborating with surrounding communities, Bacon was able to retain her mother tongue, and after moving to Tiohtià:ke Montréal, she became a translator and transcriber for anthropologists interviewing Innu Elders and Knowledge Keepers in Labrador and Québec. This work led Bacon into collaborations with documentary filmmakers Arthur Lamothe and Gilles Carle. She directed the films *Ameshkuatan – Les sorties du castor* (1978) and *Tshishe Mishtikuashisht – Le petit grand européen: Johan Beetz* (1997), and in television she collaborated on a number of series, including *Innu-Assi* (1999) and *Carcajou Mikun, Finding Our Talk* (2008). Her longstanding commitment to linguistic and cultural preservation also led her to work as a community researcher, curator, and songwriter.

Bacon is the author of several widely acclaimed collections of poetry, including *Un thé dans la toundra/Nipishapui nete mushuat* (2013), *Nous sommes tous des sauvages* (with José Acquelin, 2011) and *Bâtons à message/Tshissinuatshitakana* (2009). She has been invited to read her poems worldwide and has received many prestigious awards, including the Indigenous Voices Award, the international Ostana Prize (for writers whose mother tongue is a language of limited diffusion), and the Prix des libraires du Québec. She has been shortlisted for the Governor General's Literary Award for Poetry and the Grand Prix du livre de Montréal, received an honorary doctorate from Université Laval in 2016, and been inducted into the Ordre de Montréal and the Ordre des arts et des lettres du Québec. She is also the subject of the documentary film *Je m'appelle humain* (Call Me Human), by Kim O'Bomsawin. Bacon was awarded the Canada Council for the Arts Molson Prize for her literary contributions in 2023, the same year she was appointed as an Officer of the Order of Canada.

About her poetry, Joséphine Bacon has said, "The poems I write are for those to come, so that they do not forget their origins in a Land that will recognize their footsteps."